AGING DOG

MIRIAM FIELDS-BABINEAU

Photo credits: Miriam Fields-Babineau, Michael Calabrese, Wil de Veer, Isabelle Francais, Alice Pantfoeder, Liz Palika, Robert Pearcy, Adrienne Rescinio, Karen Taylor

© T.F.H. Publications, Inc.

Distributed in the UNITED STATES to the Pet Trade by T.F.H. Publications, Inc., 1 TFH Plaza, Neptune City, NJ 07753; on the Internet at www.tfh.com; in CANADA by Rolf C. Hagen Inc., 3225 Sartelon St., Montreal, Quebec H4R 1E8; Pet Trade by H & L Pet Supplies Inc., 27 Kingston Crescent, Kitchener, Ontario N2B 2T6; in ENGLAND by T.F.H. Publications, PO Box 74, Havant PO9 5TT; in AUSTRALIA AND THE SOUTH PACIFIC by T.F.H. (Australia), Pty. Ltd., Box 149, Brookvale 2100 N.S.W., Australia; in NEW ZEALAND by Brooklands Aquarium Ltd., 5 McGiven Drive, New Plymouth, RD1 New Zealand; in SOUTH AFRICA by Rolf C. Hagen S.A. (PTY.) LTD., P.O. Box 201199, Durban North 4016, South Africa; in JAPAN by T.F.H. Publications, Japan—Jiro Tsuda, 10-12-3 Ohjidai, Sakura, Chiba 285, Japan. Published by T.F.H. Publications, Inc.
MANUFACTURED IN THE
UNITED STATES OF AMERICA
BY T.F.H. PUBLICATIONS, INC.

An older dog can be a joy to have around and many people thrive on the canine-human relationship.

CONTENTS

A dog is a lifelong responsibility—and a lifelong friend.

THE GOLDEN YEARS

Your dog, Max, has gone through the puppy stages. Your house is no longer soiled. Your furniture is no longer used as a chew bone, and you aren't being dragged around the neighborhood. Max is in his prime. He's fun to be with, whether you share a quiet walk in the woods or cuddle in front of a fire. You can take him traveling and not have to worry about anything, other than the fact that he wants to keep going.

You know each other well.

He nudges and licks you when you don't feel good, and you're concerned for him when he's under the weather. Max may be your only child or one of many, but he is very important and you want to make sure he lives a long and healthy life.

While you watch him sleeping, playing with his doggy buddies, or eating a hearty meal, you might wonder how much longer he will be a part of your life. You are saddened that dogs don't have the same life span

as people and wonder how you can expand the limited time you have together. While there are a few things you have no control over, there are aspects of Max's life that your loving care can influence. Genetics is the one thing that you cannot control. If he comes from short-lived parents, then he, too, may have a short life. If his genetic line is susceptible to specific diseases, then there isn't much you can do, other than give him normal preventive care.

Your older dog has been a valued family member for a long time, and as a responsible owner, you will want to ensure that he enjoys good health and a quality lifestyle.

With proper diet, exercise, preventative health care, and lots of love and attention, your dog's life can be enhanced and, in some cases, even prolonged.

As his body begins to slow down, an aging dog will require more of your time and your patience.

You do have control, however over much of Max's everyday health care and overall well-being. Through proper diet, exercise, a loving environment, preventative medicine, and proper grooming, you can even prolong the life of a dog that may be prone to specific dysfunction. If Max is a member of a breed that is prone to ear infections, which can cause deafness, proper ear cleaning can decrease the possibility of age-related deafness. Or, if Max's genetic inclination is susceptible to tooth problems, which can create organ dysfunction, keeping him on a proper dental program can often prevent this from happening.

An aging dog does require more of your time than when he was younger. As his body slows down, he'll also need your patience. Age-related illnesses require frequent veterinary visits, administration of medications, and supplements. He needs your close observation, understanding, and special care. The quality of his life is up to you.

Dogs are living longer than ever due to improved medical care, nutrition, and owner education. One of the most important aspects to ensure

Plenty of exercise and stimulation will help your dog live longer. An active dog will overcome physical problems easier and will regain his health after illness faster than an inactive dog.

that Max lives longer is to offer him plenty of exercise and stimulation. A happy dog overcomes physical problems easier and regains his health after injury or surgery much faster.

While Max's length of life can be enhanced by you, it still depends on many factors. Breed and size are the two major differences. According to Bonnie Wilcox, D.V.M. and Chris Walkowicz in their book, *Old Dogs Old Friends*, dogs age most quickly during their initial year and then approximately four years for every one human year. Their comparison is as follows:

HUMAN YEARS	DOG YEARS
6 months	10 years
8 months	13 years
10 months	14 years
12 months	15 years
18 months	20 years
2 years	24 years
4 years	32 years
6 years	40 years
8 years	48 years
10 years	56 years
12 years	64 years
14 years	72 years
16 years	80 years

As you can see, while dogs age quickly during their first year, their physical aging slows down once they reach maturity, but speeds up again when they reach senior status. Can you imagine how spry a dog of 14 years must be in order to play fetch? That would be similar to a 72-year-old man playing a rigorous game of tennis!

The American Kennel Club classifies a dog of seven or older as senior. This

Your dog's size and breed type are factors that will contribute to the aging process, but with good nutrition and health care, most dogs can surpass their life expectancies.

LIFE SPAN ACCORDING TO SIZE		
Size of Dog	*Average Life Span*	*Breed Examples*
Small	Upward of 15 years of age	Yorkshire Terriers Miniature and Toy Poodles Pomeranians Shih Tzu small Terriers
Medium	12 to 14 years of age	Cocker Spaniels English Springer Spaniels Keeshonden Norwegian Elkhounds Australian Shepherds
Large	10 to 12 years of age	German Shepherds Labrador Retrievers Golden Retrievers Rottweilers Irish Setters
Giant	8 to 10 years of age	Great Danes Saint Bernards Newfoundlands Great Pyrenees Bloodhounds

A medium-sized breed like the Cocker Spaniel is considered geriatric by approximately 10 years of age, but if well cared for, can live up to 15 years. This Cocker and his friend celebrate a happy fifteenth birthday.

and individual within the breed than an overall norm. Size has much to do with life span. Another factor is genetics. Well-bred dogs with parents that have cleared health standards are likely to live longer, healthier lives. If Max's parents or grandparents live to a ripe old age, you can be pretty sure Max will as well.

The length of a dog's life can also be related to his weight. The more he weighs, the sooner the onset of geriatric condition and the shorter the life span. Through a veterinary survey in *Old Dogs, Old Friends*, it specifies that dogs that weigh less than 20 pounds are considered geriatric by the age of 11 and a half, give or take a year and nine months. However, many have lived to the ripe age of 18 or more. A medium-sized dog of 21 to 50 pounds is considered geriatric by the age of 10 years and two months, give or take a year and six months, but if well cared for can easily live up to 15 years of age. A large dog is considered geriatric by the age of eight years and nine months, give or take a year and four months. The giant breeds that weigh more than 90 pounds are considered geriatric by the age of seven years and five months, give or take a year and three months. A well-cared-for large dog can live a healthy happy life up to the age of 15 years, but this is very rare.

There are some very significant differences between a senior dog and one considered geriatric. A senior dog is simply aged. He still maintains the same

classification is pertinent mostly in instances which discuss when dogs are allowed to compete in trials and special classes. This does not mean that a dog over seven years of age should automatically be announced as "old" and therefore no longer allowed

to participate in activities. On the contrary, dogs remain young at heart longer if they are provided stimulation. Literally, a happy, working dog will have fewer internal problems.

The advent of geriatric physiology and behavior depends more on each breed activity level, eats hearty (although his diet will need to be adjusted), and has no age-related illnesses that must be addressed, such as kidney disease or bladder dysfunction. A senior dog can easily keep up with younger dogs. Granted, he may take a few more rest periods before joining in again later, but he does not shirk his duties as a teacher of young upstarts.

A geriatric dog is one that has age-related feebleness and ailments. He is on medications, has to receive special treatment, and must not be bustled about because his system has become sensitive. Most geriatric dogs have advanced arthritis. After lying down for long periods, they have difficulty getting up. They walk stiffly, eat slowly, and sleep most of the time in a quiet, dark place.

Regardless of breed characteristics or size, a well-cared-for dog will live longer. No matter what the age, a dog should be offered the same activities and maintain the same habits throughout his life. Yes, Max may be 10 or 12 years of age, but he doesn't realize that. To him, life is still full of fun and games, chances to play fetch, or runs through the woods. Provided he can maintain the same energy level and not return home breathing heavily, you can continue to allow and encourage exercise.

One of the ways to ensure that Max remains energized and happy is to have at least one other dog that is somewhat younger living with him. The younger dog

will give him more exercise and, if you tend to be away from home a lot, keep him company. This does not mean, however, that when Max reaches the geriatric stage and needs much rest and quiet that you suddenly bring in a bouncing puppy. If this is the case, then Max

should be offered some time alone away from the mischievous youngster, especially during mealtimes and bedtime.

Some of the most common geriatric conditions are cataracts, deafness, stiffness, halitosis (bad breath), senility,

A closed-off, safe environment, like a crate lined with a blanket and filled with toys, will allow your dog to spend some quiet time alone if he wishes.

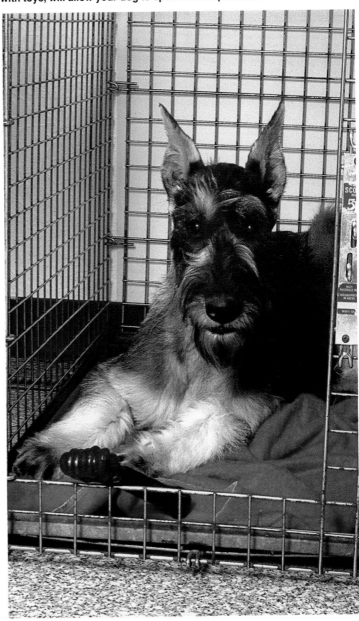

The nutritional requirements of the aging dog are significantly different than that of a puppy or an adult. Pet shops offer a variety of specially designed senior diets that will keep your old friend feeling his best. Photo courtesy of Nutro Products, Inc.

constipation or diarrhea, organ failure, and degenerative disc disease. Arthritis will affect more dogs when they reach senior status, and the disease will continue to degenerate as the dog ages.

While a senior dog may be experiencing age-related organ breakdown, he will not show any outward signs of disease until it is very advanced. There are some special signs you can look for in order to consider Max geriatric. Keep in mind, however, that this does not mean you should reduce his exercise or change how you interact with him. He will make most of these changes on his own.

The first thing you'll notice is a graying of Max's muzzle and thinning of his coat. Max's skin may thicken or get darker. He may develop calluses on his elbows. While some dogs show muzzle grayness as young as

four years of age (usually seen in larger breeds), others won't show it until they reach 12 years of age.

Another thing you'll notice as Max ages is that his eyes are

As long as you take the special needs of your aging dog into consideration, he will still remain a loving and faithful companion.

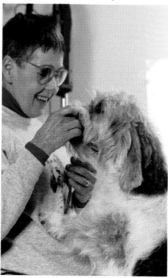

getting cloudy. This is the first sign of cataracts. His eyesight will become poor. You'll notice this most in dim light, when Max may bump into things or not be able to find you. It takes many years for full cataracts to develop, but they are easily removed, offering full eyesight for an old dog.

Hearing loss is also a common sign of aging. At first, Max's response to sounds will be selective, such as not responding to your voice command when it's time to come inside. One of the last sounds he'll ignore is the sound of his supper dish. Yes, this does seem as though Max has decided food is more important than you, but this is not entirely due to his tuning you out. Hearing degenerates gradually through the decreased ability of response to specific frequencies. Usually the higher or lower tones go first.

Max's appearance will also change with age. The muscles over his head, neck, back, and thighs will relax, making him appear a little droopy or narrow through the hips. He will appear stiff after vigorous exercise because arthritis is inflaming his joints. Max may limp a little from time to time.

The digestive system becomes more delicate because the kidneys and heart have to work without full function. Max may become constipated or have diarrhea occasionally. He'll eat slower and may even leave some of his food. He'll drink more water and may have to relieve himself more often. This is often due to kidney malfunction.

Moreover, Max may become more cranky than usual. A dog he used to play with may

Living with a younger dog or puppy can often re-energize an older dog, providing him with company and more opportunities to exercise.

become the victim of his aggression. Max will want to sleep in the same place at the same time. He'll want to go out at the same time. He won't want to be disturbed while resting. Older dogs prefer and need to maintain their schedules. They don't understand why they are feeling tired or achy and tend to become nervous or aggressive toward change.

Max may be slowing down and you will have to be careful of approaching him while he sleeps, but he is still a loyal and loving companion. He's the dog you always wanted. You no longer have to worry about coming home to a mess when you leave him home alone. Max can go with you when you travel and he enjoys a quiet evening in the den.

While Max can be classified as a senior dog by the age of seven or eight, he still has many good years left. The amount of quality time depends on you. Changing his food according to his new nutritional needs is very important, as is being more observant of his behavior. Keeping up with proper grooming will maintain your bond and allow you to monitor many physiological changes such as tumors, skin irritations, and other illnesses that cause a coat to dry out or become flaky. Regular yearly trips to the veterinarian for a physical exam and chemical blood analysis will most possibly catch any internal problems and treat them quickly.

If Max has a handicap, he'll need extra care. If he

Giant breeds like the Newfoundland have a shorter life span than smaller breeds and need special care in their later years.

can't see well, you'll need to be his eyes and guide him around obstructions. Also, make sure you don't change your furniture around. If he is unable to hear you calling him inside, try flicking lights on and off, or stomping on the ground to create vibrations.

There are many problems that Max can live with and still maintain a good quality of life—provided you are there to help. His love is very important to you and you are very important to him. Your loving care and patience will surely make his last years golden.

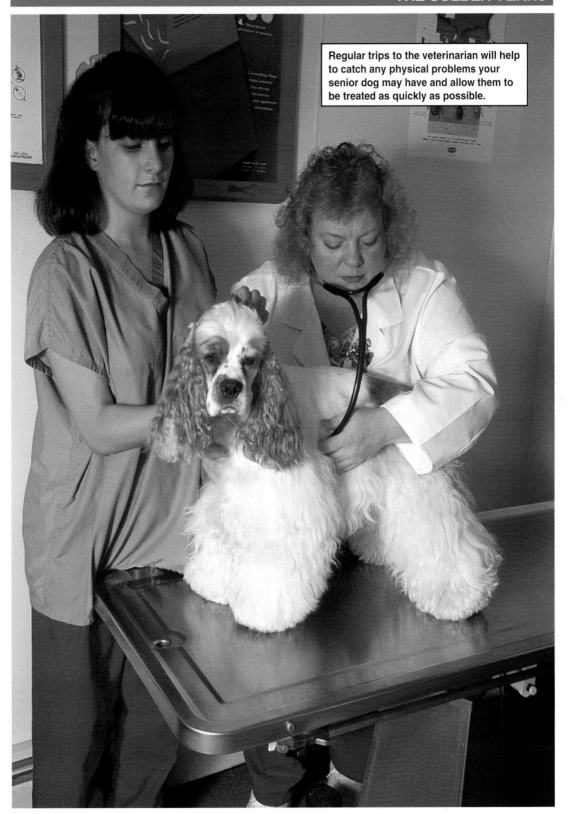

Regular trips to the veterinarian will help to catch any physical problems your senior dog may have and allow them to be treated as quickly as possible.

No matter what your dog's age may be, love, care, and attention will help to keep him young at heart.

BEHAVIORAL CHANGES

Your dog's behavior may change as he ages. He may become less excitable and prefer sleeping to strenuous exercise or playtime.

Your dog's body takes a beating throughout his life. Muscles are pulled, joints stressed, and organs scarred by infection. Cell structure breaks down, decreasing the efficacy of organs and tissues. All of these traumas cause abnormal cell development, which in turn create tumors and arthritic conditions.

On the outside, Max can appear as healthy and active as any younger dog, but inside his organs are not functioning as efficiently as when he was younger. For example, if the kidneys begin to deteriorate, they can continue to function with only 40 percent of the tubules (the part of the kidney that breaks down nutrients from urea) working. Max will continue feeling fine and behaving normally. However, this can take a quick turn for the worse if a kidney disease continues to deteriorate. This can happen slowly or what seems like overnight. Until this happens, the only difference in Max will be his need to urinate more often. Otherwise, there is no sign of a problem.

As Max ages, we need to ensure his complete health by adjusting his diet, exercise, and by keeping a close watch on his behavior. In fact, you'll notice many problems first through behavioral changes before his body shows the outward signs.

Changes in appetite, a lack of desire to move about, or overall grouchiness are usually symptoms of a deeper problem.

Max's muscles will remain strong, provided he exercises. The more he does as a youngster, the more he can do as an oldster. You must keep in mind, however, that Max cannot tell you he doesn't want to go those extra miles with you. All he wants is to be with you and please you, regardless of how he feels. His muscles may still be strong at this point, but his internal workings are no longer operating in prime condition. Max can still remain physically healthy with a little less exercise—maybe

Lots of activity may be stressful to your aging dog. Children should still show him affection, but allow him plenty of time alone as well.

two or three miles instead of five or maybe you can do the run on softer ground instead of hard concrete.

The musculoskeletal system will usually exhibit arthritic changes as Max turns into a senior dog. Arthritis is formed through changes in the joint bones, a reduction of cartilage, and a thickening of the synovial fluid between the joints. Often, inflammation can cause more irritation and lameness.

Not only will the arthritic changes cause pain in the joints, but they will also cause atrophy in the muscles because Max will not want to move around. The muscles begin to get loose and hang off the bones. This is most obvious along the spine, chest, and hind legs. As the muscles

atrophy, the skin will appear looser or baggy.

Overall, Max becomes a different dog as his senior years take over. He moves more slowly, picks at his meals, and may bump into things that he can't see. However, the biggest change will be in his behavior.

As Max ages, he may not only slow down, he will also become less excitable in general. He will still greet you with a wagging tail, but not jump on you or perform aerial leaps when you come home. When going out, he'll walk to the door and wait patiently as you search for his leash—no more racing in circles, barking excitedly, and jumping about.

As they mature, dogs become less tolerant of changes. This can be due to an internal dysfunction, sensory

loss, or simply age-related senility. If Max suffers from sight loss, he will not acclimate well to environmental changes, such as moving the furniture around or a move to a new home.

A dog suffering hearing loss will also have a difficult time if moved into a new environment. Not only will balance be affected, many dogs have a difficult time knowing where they are. Some will become lost in their own homes. This can also occur to a dog that has lost his sense of smell.

Older dogs also need to have a quiet place to sleep. Activity can be stressful and living with young children offers a geriatric dog little relief form overexuberant attention. Yes, Max should receive love and attention, but he also needs

Adding another dog to your household can provide your older dog with necessary stimulation, but his senior status should always be respected.

time alone to rest. He'll be much happier in his job as a foot warmer than as an activity coordinator.

You will need to maintain established routines, such as consistent feeding and walking times. Max needs to know what happens and when. A stress as simple as confusion about when he's going to eat can cause an organ dysfunction, because the stress causes the immune system to weaken. As he ages he'll need to relieve himself more often; therefore, he'll need to go out more. Having to contain himself for longer periods of time can in itself cause kidney or bladder

Senior dogs like to maintain a regular schedule of eating, sleeping, and eliminating. Establishing routines will provide comfort to your dog.

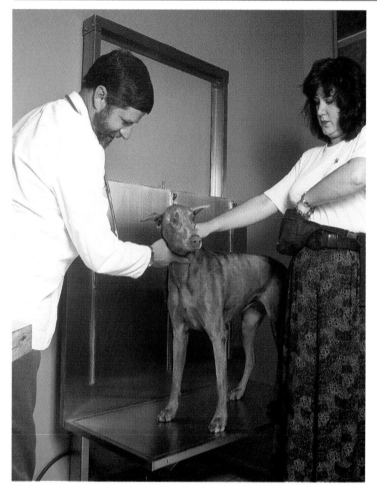

A sudden change in your dog's behavior may indicate a health-related problem. Take your older dog to the veterinarian first to rule out any physical reasons for his misbehavior before trying to correct him.

become more insistent on getting their own way. This especially happens if their people allow them to become sloppy in their responses to commands or let them do something one time because of an illness that they wouldn't normally do, such as lying on the couch or bed.

Dogs have an "all or none" policy. They either do it all the time or not at all. This continues to hold true for older dogs. There are no "gray" areas in the dog's psyche. They don't understand sometimes, maybe, and it's okay this time but not next time. They can either do something or not do it. When Max decides to test his parameters and not listen to a command, you'd best make him listen. For example, you tell him to sit and he doesn't listen. Instead of repeating your command, make him sit. If he begins to sneak up on the couch at night, he'll need to be corrected or confined to prevent the bad behavior.

A multi-dog household will require other changes to accommodate Max. First of all, his senior dog status means that he should also be treated as top dog. This means that he is fed first, played with or worked first and, if both dogs come to you at the same time for attention, Max is pet first. Max should be allowed his special place, closest to your side. The younger dogs will have their turns, so don't feel badly.

It'll be natural for two dominant dogs to quarrel from time to time. You will need to be sure that the younger dog is corrected for his behavior, allowing Max to "win." In general, Max is to receive preferential treatment over the other younger dogs.

problems. Relieving himself in the house when he knows how "bad" it is will cause extreme anxiety and stress.

Older dogs also prefer to wake and sleep at the same time of the day. You'll find yourself awakened by a wet nose at the same time every morning and stared at until you get up. Max is better than any alarm clock. Not only is he very accurate, but power failures never shut him off. Established routines are comforting to old dogs.

All dogs, young and old, prefer to know what is going to happen and when. This develops proper house manners and keeps their people in line. Keep in mind that dogs aren't always aware of the changes that occur with weekends and holidays. Despite the fact that he enjoys your company, these times can be disruptive to an old dog. Try to maintain the same "happening" hours throughout the day, every day.

Although Max has earned his right to be the top dog, this does not mean you should start to allow him to bend the rules. Many older dogs will

If Max is an only dog or has recently lost a companion, it may be a good idea to procure another dog. At first, Max may be reticent about accepting this newcomer, but eventually, it will breathe a new life into him. A youngster will make him exercise more and offer him companionship when you are away from home.

If Max is a dominant dog, you will need to introduce the new dog in a neutral territory, such as a commons or park. Any new dog is accepted easier if it is of the opposite sex and/or very young, such as a puppy. Older dogs will put up with more indiscretions from puppies than they will from another older dog. As the puppy ages, he will learn his "place." Older dogs will teach proper social skills to younger ones. These lessons are very important for the younger dog's own behavioral skills.

A sudden change in behavior such as pacing, whining, or sudden aggression can mean a physical problem. Max should be taken to the veterinarian as soon as possible and given a complete physical and blood test. If the veterinarian gives him a clean bill of health, then the problem could be solely behavioral, meaning he is bored or jealous and needs to be given a purpose in life. This can be done through obedience training, teaching him tricks, or just taking a special walk with him each day.

Often, a sudden onset of aggression without provocation does mean an internal dysfunction. Tumors can cause biochemical changes, which in turn lead to aggression and short temper. Pain will cause sudden aggressive eruptions

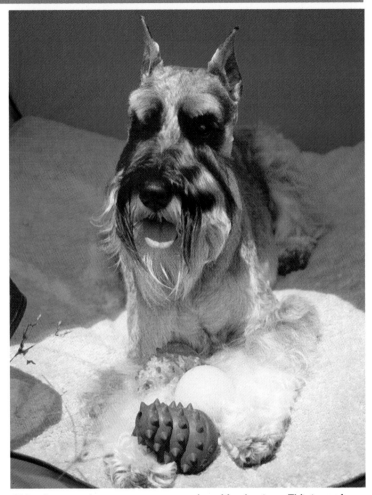

Older dogs may become more possessive of food or toys. This type of behavior should not be tolerated.

if the affected area is touched or manipulated. Misundertanding a situation can also cause aggression. For example, a dog that cannot hear is suddenly awakened from a deep sleep. He may snap before realizing he had been touched by his beloved person.

Many older dogs also become more possessive as they age. This can mean displaying aggression toward strangers that walk in the door or even toward family members who wish to take away a special bone or toy. In all these instances, Max should be corrected. He needs to know that people will always come first and that aggression is not acceptable, regardless of the situation.

Patience will be needed as Max ages. You must maintain his schedules, a proper diet, exercise, and stimulation. Keep him involved in your life. While many of Max's emotional changes are due to dysfunction, more often than not they can also be due to his not receiving enough exercise and attention.

All of us need to feel that we are needed. Dogs are no different.

As your dog reaches senior status, he will require daily grooming to keep his coat healthy and looking its best.

GOOD HEALTH
FOR A LONG LIFE

The most important aspect of maintaining Max's health and ensuring that he lives a long time is to offer him the proper nutrition, care, and exercise that benefit a dog of his stature and years. As Max ages, his body requires a different type of nutrition. His coat will need more careful maintenance and, as aging slows down his energy level, you will need to encourage him to exercise, offering new activities that won't stress his system. You will also need to change both his and your lifestyle to accommodate his needs.

GROOMING

Grooming is one of the many things you can attend to

Not only is grooming a great way to spend time with your dog, it also gives you an opportunity to check his coat and skin for any problems.

at home. As dogs reach senior status, they require daily grooming. Many older dogs will become less than fragrant and, if they have long hair, detritus will cling to orifices, causing worse odor and possible infection. Some dogs may object to being groomed more often and may even cry out when you attend to things such as nail clipping or ear cleaning.

Regardless of Max's reaction, you need to make sure he remains clean and in the peak of health. Do a daily check up while you groom him. Not only will you be spending quality time with him, grooming will give Max a shiny, healthy coat, and if there is a problem, you may be able to discover it sooner.

Some dogs will need to be taken care of by a professional groomer. As Max ages, you may want to forgo the fancy cuts and settle for something more simple. A long-haired dog might benefit from having his fur reduced to one or two inches, because it cuts down on detritus getting stuck in his fur and allows you to discover lumps easier. Many dogs actually feel better without all the tangles and weight of a long coat.

DENTAL CARE

Part of your dog's grooming regimen should include cleaning his teeth. As dogs age, their teeth wear down and tend to collect tartar faster, causing gingivitis and other

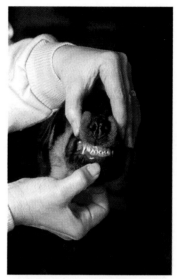

Good dental care will result in your dog's teeth lasting longer and will help him maintain a healthy appetite and overall good health.

bacterial diseases that can cause organ dysfunction. While a daily cleaning would be ideal, at least try to attend to this twice per week. Scaling the teeth every so often will also be helpful in keeping down the tartar build-up. Regular dental attention will mean Max's teeth will last longer, allowing him to chew better, which also means he'll maintain a healthy appetite and overall good health.

Dental problems are characterized by bad breath, tartar build-up around the gums, bleeding gums, and in real bad cases, pus leakage around the gums and loose teeth. The only way to slow down the wearing out of Max's teeth is to maintain good dental practices.

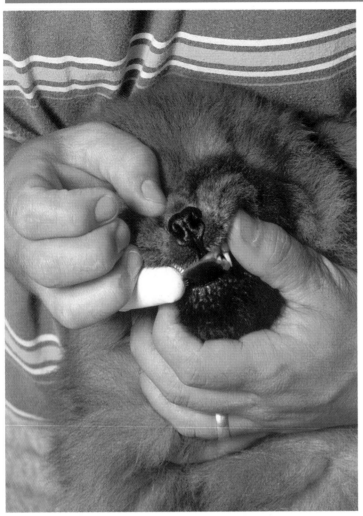

Using a soft cloth wrapped around your index finger and toothpaste made especially for dogs, you can clean your dog's teeth on a daily basis.

rubbing off excess plaque and distributing the toothpaste more evenly throughout the jaw. Turn this into part of your daily grooming routine so that you never forget.

VETERINARY CARE

Another important factor in maintaining a healthy oldster is to make sure your dog gets annual booster shots, checkups, and blood tests. The boosters maintain his resistance to infectious diseases. This is especially important if Max is exposed to other dogs, either while traveling, going on regular visits to a park where he plays with other dogs, or if left in a kennel.

Older dogs have less powerful immune systems and therefore cannot fight infection as easily as a younger dog. However, the healthier Max is, the easier he'll fight infections. Yearly checkups will inform you of any changes in Max's health, such as a sensory disability. A blood test will let

A thorough oral exam should be a part of your dog's regular veterinary visit.

If your dog is not used to having his teeth done, your veterinarian will need to attend to his teeth first. The veterinarian will carefully scale all the tartar off his teeth and polish them to protect from further tartar build-up. Once this is done, make it a regular practice to brush Max's teeth using toothpaste that is specially formulated for dogs. Doggy toothpaste doesn't have the same foaming agent found in people toothpaste and comes in more inviting flavors, such as beef, liver, and chicken. Once Max gets a taste of that, his brushing time will turn into treat time!

Begin teaching Max to accept his dental attention by using a soft cloth wrapped around your index finger. Dampen it with warm water and apply about a half of a teaspoon of toothpaste. Using circular motions, rub each of his teeth in turn, reapplying the toothpaste as needed. Once Max is used to this process, use a finger brush with soft rubber bristles. These will do a better job of

Your dog can pick up all kinds of parasites in the great outdoors. Be sure to check your dog's coat carefully for fleas and ticks that may cause infections or allergic reactions.

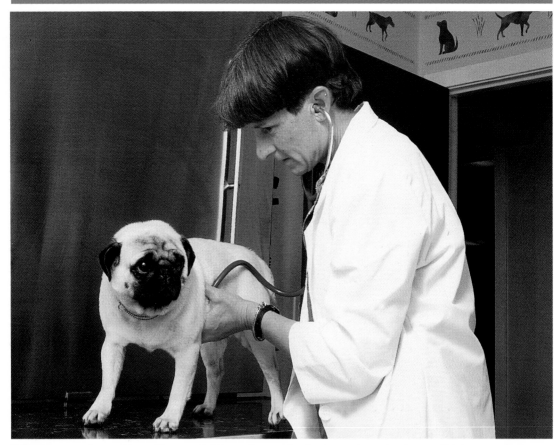

Make sure your dog continues his annual visits to the veterinarian to receive a checkup and his booster shots.

you know how his organs and immune system are holding up. Most dysfunctions, such as kidney and liver diseases, cancer, and parasitic infestations, will show up in the blood test. Even if Max is 100 percent healthy, it's a good idea to have a blood test to serve as a base line against future tests. This way, your veterinarian will be better prepared for an emergency, and he'll also know when something is not normal during a regular checkup.

Parasite control is of the utmost importance in an old dog. As with other infections, he cannot withstand infestation without becoming very sick. Fleas will cause allergic reactions, such as thickening of the skin, hair loss, and internal parasites like tapeworms. You must also be aware that the repeated dipping and spraying of insecticides will harm his liver. Therefore, it's imperative to maintain a flea-free environment through prevention. A monthly flea preventative, either oral or topical, will prevent infestation. Giving Max Brewer's Yeast and garlic will help to repel the bugs, as well as benefit his coat and digestive system.

Roundworm can also be a threat to older dogs. While these worms are most prevalent in puppies and nursing mothers, they can also be present in an older dog's bowels. Infestation is easily

Parasite control is very important when dealing with an older dog. Regular grooming will help you stop infestation problems before they start.

Spaying or neutering your dog when young will help him avoid many health problems that can occur with old age.

prevented through a regular biannual stool check. Bring a sample of your dog's feces to your veterinarian and have it analyzed every six months. Roundworm may not cause a severe reaction, but can be damaging because it reduces Max's ability to fight other infections.

Whipworm and hookworm can be very damaging to older dog's weakened immune systems. Both worms can cause diarrhea, vomiting, loss of appetite and, if the infestation is not promptly treated, it can eventually be fatal. These parasites can also be identified through a fecal analysis.

External parasites such as ticks and lice should also be curbed. Ticks can cause skin irritations, rashes, and the dreaded Lyme disease, which can cripple your dog. The best preventative is a topical tick deterrent and regular checkups, especially during the spring and early summer. Ticks prefer warm, moist places, such as the ears, eyes, under the legs, and along the spine, which is where they drop onto dogs from foliage.

Lice can cause skin irritations and reduce immune system response to bacterial invasion. Due to the fact that lice live their entire lives on animals, you'll most

often see this problem in kenneled dogs. Lice appear as little whitish dots on the dog's fur. They cause extreme skin irritation and can lead to secondary infections. Lice can easily be treated with two or three insecticidal baths and by cleaning the dog's bedding.

Probably the most important thing you can do for your older dog is to have him neutered. This will prevent many problems later in life, such as cancers of the reproductive systems, breast cancer, and hernias. Overall, Max will be a healthier dog and better pet after being neutered. There are just a few considerations about

Your dog's nutritional requirements will change as he ages. His metabolism will slow down and his appetite may lessen.

It may also become necessary to feed Max three smaller meals per day instead of one or two large ones, in order to allow his system to properly absorb and metabolize the nutrients. This is helpful for dogs with disorders of the liver or kidneys. If Max does not wish to eat, like many older dogs with a reduced ability to smell, warming the food may help with palatability. You can also let dry food soak in salt and sugar-free chicken bullion. This enhances the ease of chewing and promotes more flavor.

Vitamins will play an important part in Max's health. He'll need supplements added to his food that supply extra Vitamin B to perpetuate his metabolism and appetite, Vitamins A and E for his muscles and eyes, and fatty acids to maintain a glossy coat. The nutriceuticals glycosamine, sulfate, and chondroitin will also help maintain joint and bone health, often relieving symptoms of arthritis. There are many commercial foods that already have these nutrients, but offering a daily chewable vitamin or a sprinkle of powder on his food ensures complete coverage.

Glycosamine sulfate and chondroitin have been hailed as the miracle cure for arthritis. It is now sold in both powder and tablet forms for both humans and animals. Ask your veterinarian which product will work best for Max. There are several made specifically for canines, but all require long term usage. If you resort to using this product, you will see a change in Max in approximately 60 days. He'll move around easier and there will be less

neutering that you should be aware of. First of all, your dog will tend to put on more weight. This is easily controlled through proper diet and exercise. Also, there is the possibility of the dog developing incontinence. This could also happen naturally with old age and, once again, proper diet and exercise will help control this problem.

NUTRITION

Max's nutritional requirements change with his age. While he needed a high-protein, high-fat diet as a puppy, heavy concentrations of these nutrients are detrimental to his health as a senior dog. As dogs age, their metabolism slows down and the ability to efficiently digest protein, sodium, sugar, and fat decreases. Dogs with internal dysfunction will need to be put on a prescription diet or one low in exacerbating components. Other factors you should consider are his appetite and his ability to chew dry food. Dogs with worn teeth or gum problems will not only prefer softer foods, but will be able to digest them better.

There are many good-quality dog foods on the market made especially for your older dog that will offer him the proper nutritional balance he requires.

inflammation around his joints.

When choosing a commercial diet, look for the following specific ingredient breakdowns as measured against 100 grams of food:

No more than 14 grams of protein;

No more than 9.5 grams of fat;

1.2 grams of fiber, or more;

Less than .28 grams of sodium;

Less than .33 grams of phosphorous;

About .55 grams of calcium.

Cutting down on sodium, fat, sugar, and potassium will help him properly digest his kibble. As Max ages, his sense of smell may decrease, making food less palatable. Adding a bit of special canned diet food will not only make him want to eat, but also will add much needed moisture to help his kidneys work. Fiber will aid the gastrointestinal tract, reducing the incidence of colitis and diarrhea associated with other dysfunction. Offering too many calcium-rich foods, such as milk or cream, not only increases Max's fat intake but also may cause digestive problems and result in diarrhea.

Regardless of the health or age of your dog, be sure to provide plenty of fresh water. This helps maintain your dog's

A constant supply of clean, cool water is essential for your dog's health, especially in his senior years.

The type of diet you choose for your dog will depend on his state of health and level of activity. Choose a food that will address your dog's special needs.

Obesity can be a problem in older dogs, so limit the amount of treats you give your dog and make sure he gets enough exercise.

hydration. Lots of water is especially important if Max has a kidney disorder, diabetes, chronic vomiting, or diarrhea. If Max stops drinking regularly, he can become dehydrated and anemic. He must go to the veterinarian immediately for intravenous fluids. Monitor his water intake to ensure he maintains his hydration level. Dogs average two liters per day of fluid intake. While much of his moisture can be obtained through moist food, he must drink the rest from his water bowl.

One of the ways to check Max's hydration level is to take a fold of his skin between your fingers, then let go. If his skin snaps back into place, he is

properly hydrated. If his skin remains loose or slowly returns to normal, he is dehydrated and will need immediate veterinary care and intravenous fluids.

Obesity is one of the biggest problems facing an elderly dog. An obese dog can develop any number of internal disorders that can be detrimental to his overall health and shorten his life. While dogs age, their slowing metabolism will cause a decreased rate of fat digestion, absorbing more into their intestines and other tissues. This strains the heart, kidneys, bones, and muscles. Through weight maintenance, you control your dog's quality and length of life. There are several simple ways of keeping Max's weight at optimum levels and, to Max's relief, this often does not involve offering less food. There are special diets on the market that are specially formulated for senior dogs, offering the proper nutritional balance.

The type of diet you choose should depend on Max's state of health. If Max is underweight due to an underlying disease, he may need a higher calorie diet, whereas an overweight dog needs a lower calorie diet. The best means of knowing what your oldster needs is to consult with your veterinarian. A thorough physical, including a blood test, will draw a baseline, informing you of Max's dietary needs.

You can often tell just by looking at your dog whether or not he is overweight. There should be some waistline between his lower ribs and his hips. If you see no change or even an enlargement in this area, Max is overweight. Max's stomach should not distend below the knees of his hind legs. Again, there should be an indent from the lower part of the rib cage into the lower abdomen. Older dogs do have some relaxation of the muscles in their abdominal area, but this is easily noted as loose skin, versus the solidness of fat.

LIFESTYLE CHANGES

The type of lifestyle changes you and your dog must make

Most senior dogs can maintain the same level of activity as they did when younger, but if your dog develops any age-related conditions, he will have to be accommodated.

Your older dog may suffer separation anxiety or stress when you leave him alone. Try to keep him as comfortable as possible and bring him with you whenever you can.

stroke. If it happens again, he'll need immediate attention.

While older dogs sleep most of the day and wait for you to come home, some can become anxious or develop separation anxiety. This happens most often if they have a health problem—dogs with health problems sometimes tend to panic without their people around. Their anxiety can cause destructiveness or stress on their systems. The last thing you want to do is put stress on your older dog. Stress can often be the catalyst that causes decreased immune system functions. Thus, a stressed dog may become more susceptible to airborne illnesses, allergies, or internal diseases.

One of the ways to prevent stress is to keep Max in a safely enclosed environment. This place should be a room in your home where you spend much of your time, such as the kitchen or family room. This way, Max can feel comfort in your odor as well as in his familiar surroundings. Sometimes a soft background noise will help. Turn on the radio or television, keeping the volume low. Remember, dogs can hear twice as well as we can. Even older dogs retain this ability. The sounds of voices can be soothing.

Make sure Max's enclosure is warm, has a soft bed, and he is provided with plenty of fresh water. A window to look out of is helpful. Dogs love to people watch. If Max is a hunting dog, bird watching can be pretty entertaining as well.

GETTING A NEW FRIEND

Young children or puppies can also be stressful to an old

depends on your dog's personality and health. Most senior dogs are well adjusted, get along fine at home alone for long periods of time, and can still run and play as much as before. However, as Max moves into geriatric condition and develops the inevitable age-related problems, he will need to be accommodated. This can mean anything from a simple slowing down of activities to housing changes.

If Max develops a dysfunction that requires having to relieve himself often,

he will need to be allowed access to a relief area. Ideally, you should install a doggy door and teach Max how to use it. The other thing you can do if you are away from home for long periods of time is obtain the services of a dog walker or a neighbor to check on Max and let him out one or two times during the day. Whomever you hire should have the veterinarian's phone number, as well as your work number. This is especially important if Max has experienced a seizure or

Young children may stress out older dogs unintentionally. Good basic training and plenty of one-on-one time between you and your dog should help prevent problems from occurring.

As long as they are properly introduced, the bond between a child and his canine companion can be a strong one.

Older dogs have special nutritional requirements. There are dog foods available that contain high-quality ingredients and are modified to better meet the senior dog's decreased protein and energy requirements. Photo courtesy of Eight in One Pet Products.

dog. This often occurs when the dog has been the "baby" of the family for most of his life and all of a sudden, along comes a puppy or infant. The youngster takes up much of your time, leaving Max without the attention he used to receive. Not only that, but when the baby begins to crawl around, he enters Max's personal space!

In the case of a human infant, many older dogs will become cranky. This can manifest itself as anything from destructiveness to aggressive behavior. You are left in a quandary, not wanting to get rid of Max, yet not wanting to threaten the safety of your infant. Often, the cranky old dog is tearfully sent to the pound, and, because most people do not want an old dog, he ends up being put to sleep.

This can often be prevented if you prepare Max for the infant's arrival. The process begins with basic obedience training. If Max went through the training when he was a puppy, then refresh his memory with another series of classes and, this time, keep up with it. Max needs his individual time each day. That means your undivided attention for at least 30 minutes. Practicing obedience work is not only fun for Max, but is also a constructive use of your time with him. He learns to listen to you and you both get some exercise.

If you have allowed Max to jump on you or the furniture, he'll need to learn to stop these behaviors. Jumping up can be dangerous to an infant. Using sound and basic consistency, Max can learn to stop jumping up. No matter how old Max is,

Owning a dog can teach a child respect and love for animals. Once your dog gets used to the children in your household, he will be more than happy to join in the fun.

he is never too old to learn new things. Yes, old dogs can learn new tricks! In fact, they enjoy the stimulation.

To keep Max from jumping up, the easiest and most humane means of teaching him is to use a "No Jump Box." This consists of 15 pennies in a small tin or metal (not aluminum) box. You may want to make several boxes and place them in strategic areas around the house, such as in the kitchen, near doors, and in the family room.

When Max jumps up, shake the can in an up-and-down motion once or twice as you reprimand him in a low tone of voice. The sound will startle Max. He'll either run a short distance away or sit and look at you. Either response should be praised. Max must know to keep all four feet on the floor. Be certain to always praise him if he comes to you and sits for attention. This encourages appropriate behavior.

House rules will need to be changed as well. This means that everyone in the house must not allow Max to break the rules. If this occurs, Max will become frustrated and defensive. Be consistent. It's the key to reliability and understanding. All of you will be far happier.

Long before the infant's arrival, Max will need to be acclimated to the sounds and smells of babies. Take him to parks where children play and to friends' houses that have babies and/or children. Make him work the entire time that he is presented with these distractions. If he is friendly and minds his manners, allow him time to interact with the youngsters.

Practice the sit and down/stay command as children run past. He'll also need to walk around bouncing youngsters and learn to ignore their erratic sounds and motions. Always praise him as he

Older dogs may lose patience with rambunctious young puppies. Be sure to supervise them when they are together to keep both dogs safe. This pup tries to get the attention of his senior friend.

Introduce your older dog to any new members of the family—canine or human—very carefully. This will ensure a good start to the new relationship.

watches you and as he performs his commands. He'll learn to associate the children with the fun of working, making it a far more pleasant experience for everyone.

Prepare Max for your new baby by taking him into the nursery and letting him sniff the cradle, changing table, and diaper pail. Make him perform the stay command in the room as you walk around. This will prepare him for those times when you are changing diapers or lulling Junior to sleep. Max will know his role.

Begin decreasing the attention you give Max. Most of your time will be taken up with baby chores, more so as the baby ages and becomes mobile. Remember that Max

has been your baby for a long time, demanding attention whenever he chose. Max must learn that he'll only receive attention when you wish to give it. This means that when you are seated on the couch or rocking chair he is not to paw at or jump up on you to demand petting. He must be ignored or corrected until you choose to pet him.

You can practice this by holding a baby blanket in your arms and sitting down. Each time Max demands attention, shove him away and reprimand him in a low tone of voice. Before sitting you can offer him a chew toy to occupy him, but don't play with him. If he becomes persistent, place him in a

down/stay at your feet or nearby. No matter how many times he pops up, replace him. Working will keep him occupied and happy.

When the baby arrives, Max will need to be properly introduced. Keeping the infant entirely away from him will only cause more anxiety. On the first day, place Max in a sit/stay near a chair or couch. Sit on the couch holding your baby. Max will be so curious his head will strain to catch Junior's scent. As he remains in his stay position, praise him.

When he becomes calm, release him from his stay but have someone holding his leash. Allow him to put his

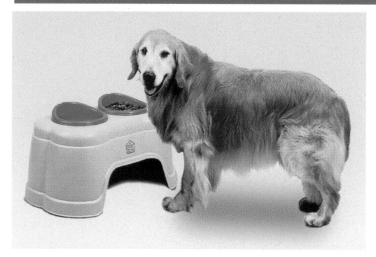

Proper nutrition is imperative to your dog's health. Veterinarians recommend elevated feeders to help reduce stress on your dog's neck and back muscles. The raised platform also provides better digestion while reducing bloating and gas. Photo courtesy of Pet Zone Products, Ltd.

nose next to the infant. As long as he remains calm, the leash should remain loose. Praise him for his good behavior and offer him a treat. This gives him a positive association with the baby. If Max becomes impatient and tries to jump up, the person holding the leash should tug it back and reprimand him in a low tone of voice. Be careful that the person holding the leash is not nervous in any way. Max will pick up on this emotion and also become nervous. The leash must remain loose! This is of the utmost importance because a tight leash will cause Max to become aggressive and this is not the way to begin a sibling relationship.

Max should be allowed to be part of the proud parentage. Let him remain near as you feed and change your infant. Keeping him in stays and heeling him from place to place not only teaches him to remain quiet around the baby, but also works him, which keeps him happy. Now he won't be as aggressive or destructive

because he's fully aware of what is going on and how to behave.

Many dogs will become very protective of their new siblings. This, too, is to be avoided at the first sign. Never allow Max to show aggression toward anyone for any reason. Letting him growl can lead to a bite. It is not cute when Max protects your baby from other people and animals without reason. Yes, it's nice to know that he'll protect Junior from strangers, but he needs to be aware that not everyone is to be included on this roster, especially visiting friends and relatives.

Puppies can also have this effect on an old dog. While he may become more lively once he is used to the pup, he will still be protective of his territory and rights as a senior citizen. This can mean that he will display aggressive behavior when the puppy shows indiscretions, such as taking Max's favorite sleeping spot or receiving preferential petting. Yes, it's more fun to pet and cuddle a soft puppy than an

odiferous old dog, but Max doesn't see it that way. He sees his position threatened. This causes aggression toward the puppy.

If Max has any disease or dysfunction, you should never leave him with younger dogs. Not only will he tend to have a short fuse, but a tussle, whether in play or anger, can be damaging. Keep him separate from youngsters and allow him some peace. Also, offer him a place where he can "get away from it all," such as a crate in a warm, dark place. Only he should be allowed access to this spot. Keep younger dogs and children away from it.

A multi-dog household will present other considerations. One is feeding time. Older dogs tend to eat slower and usually have a special diet. Placing Max with the rest of the pack can cause problems because the younger dogs may push Max away from his food before he's finished. This can cause fighting or result in Max not fulfilling his nutritional needs. Avoid this by feeding him separately. Allow him a stress-free environment in which to eat.

Another consideration is relief time. If you have a fenced-in yard, allow Max to go out by himself. Max requires more time and quiet. He may benefit more from your taking him for a walk instead of just being let outside. This way you can allow him to go in peace and it's easier for you to keep track of his internal health by observing his actions and droppings. Loose, mucous, or bloody stool can be the first sign of an internal disorder. Straining to defecate or urinate can be another sign of dysfunction.

Traveling with your dog may become more difficult as he ages. You must take your dog's physical health and mental well-being into consideration before making plans.

Aging dogs will take up more of your time and will need your cooperation in order to continue doing things with you and your family.

Traveling with Max may become difficult as he ages. You'll need to stop more often to allow him to relieve himself. You should also consider how stressed Max might be at your destination. Will he be on another dog's territory? If so, he can be very stressed by the other dog's challenges and by simply being in an unfamiliar area. A dog with sight or hearing problems will not do well in a new place.

Extreme temperatures can also be stressful. As dogs age, they cannot conserve their body temperatures as easily as when they were young. Very hot, humid weather or very cold weather will be difficult for Max to adjust to, especially if his home is in the opposite climate.

Kenneling can also be very stressful. He is put in an unfamiliar place with lots of noise, people he doesn't know, and his family gone. If a dog in the kennel is ill, Max will be susceptible to the infection. An infestation of fleas, lice, or mange could also cause Max discomfort and secondary problems.

If you have no other choice than to kennel Max, be sure to tour the kennel and speak to the personnel before leaving him. Will Max be given his medication and special food? How often are the kennels cleaned? Is there somewhere that Max can have a walk outside? Will he have to put up with dogs sticking their noses into his kennel? Is there a veterinarian on call? These are all very important questions. They could mean the difference between life and death to an older dog.

If Max is unable to travel with you, try finding a friend or family member to take care of him while you're gone. Better yet, find someone who can either stop in at your home three times per day or actually stay with him at home. He may still be stressed without having you around, but he will be more comfortable in his own home than a strange area.

Aging dogs need more of your time and cooperation. Take a few extra minutes each day to offer Max his due. It's time to show your true loyalty and devotion to one who has idolized you his entire life. Max may not be able to get the paper any more, but he can still walk with you down the driveway. Make time for him.

COMMON AILMENTS

While there are many ways to slow down the aging process or to make certain that Max isn't affected by preventable physical ailments, there is no way for you to rebuild aged internal systems. Max's body will inevitably break down, but knowing the first signs of illness may help both you and Max overcome and prepare for life's changes.

The first things you may notice are changes in Max's senses: his eyes, hearing, and overall reaction to his environment. Close observation will yield possible changes in his appearance and mannerisms. It is important that you notify your veterinarian immediately if Max shows any abrupt change, such as not eating, vomiting, diarrhea, or trouble breathing. These symptoms can signify many different things and only your veterinarian would be able to diagnose the problem and offer treatment.

The aging process will most likely affect your dog's senses. Age-related problems can diminish your dog's eyesight and his eyes will need to be checked regularly.

SIGHT

Before you can hope to understand how a dog's senses are affected by aging, you first need to understand how they work. Let's begin with canine eyes. They were designed to perceive forms and movement instead of distinct features. Thus, they can quickly detect movement, but cannot see contours. For example, while hunting a rabbit, they can first detect it with their nose, but can only see it if it moves.

Studies have shown that a dog's visual acuity can be compared to ours during sunset. While they see some colors such as greens and yellows, they do not have as vivid a range as we do. As dogs age, the nerve sensitivity in the eyes is reduced, causing diminished sight.

Several age-related problems can cause further diminished eyesight: cataracts, glaucoma, dry eye, and retinal degeneration, which is an inherited disease.

Cataracts

The lens of the eye becomes opaque, blocking the flow of light to the retina. This may develop slowly over the course of several years and is not painful.

Symptoms: A gradual

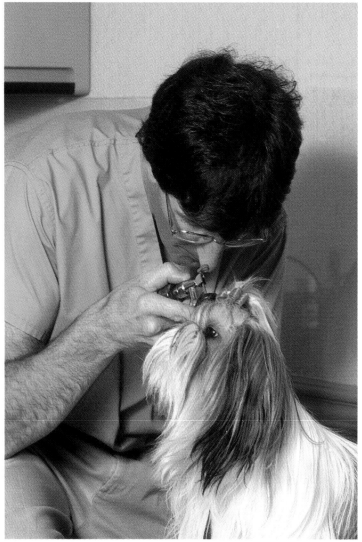

Treatments are available for some age-related eye problems. Take your dog to the veterinarian immediately if he seems to be having difficulty with his sight.

increase of haziness in eyeball. Sight slowly diminishes.

Treatment: One of the easiest eye conditions to treat. Once the cataracts have matured, they are easily removed through surgery and full eyesight is restored.

Adjustments: Due to Max's decreased eyesight, be sure to keep him in a fenced yard, walk him on a leash, feed him in the same place, and don't change your furniture around.

Glaucoma

Increase in fluid pressure within the eye. This problem can develop as a secondary dysfunction to cataracts, inflammation, and allergies. Blindness can result from retina damage.

Symptoms: Reddened and inflamed eyes with a haze about the cornea and dilated pupils.

Treatment: Reduction of eye fluid should be instituted without delay. Initially, drugs can be used to reduce the inflammation and draw the fluid out of the eye and into the bloodstream. A long-term regimen of anti-inflammatory drugs should be administered. If the drugs do not work, surgery might restore Max's eyesight. Acupuncture has also been used successfully.

Adjustments: Again, keeping Max in a fenced yard, walking him on a leash, and maintaining a regular schedule will be helpful. You will also need to remember to give him medications.

Dry Eye

This is caused by a reduction in tear production that keeps Max's eyes moist. This disease can dry the cornea, causing tissue damage and ulcerations. If left untreated, blindness results. Dry eye can be a genetic dysfunction or occur in dogs with thyroid problems, autoimmune disease, or diabetes melitis.

Symptoms: Greenish mucous discharge in and around both eyes, as well as ulcers on the surface that cause redness and pain. If this continues untreated, black spots will appear on the cornea.

Treatment: Tear replacement drops several times per day, antibiotics, and anti-inflammatory ointment is used to combat infection.

Adjustments: Don't allow Max to wander off leash. He should only be loose in a fenced-in area. Keep everything in his home the

Recognizing the signs of aging may help both you and your dog prepare for life's changes.

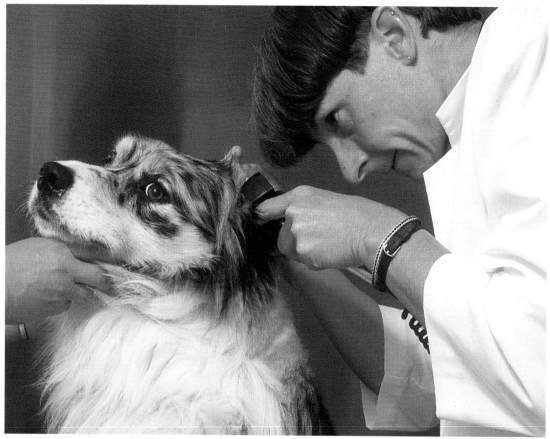

A dog's hearing will be one of the first senses that may degenerate with old age. You may have to adjust your tone of voice and be careful not to startle your dog if he is experiencing hearing loss.

same and, if you have other animals, feed him separately.

HEARING

A dog's hearing is one of the first things to degenerate with old age. Their ability to hear high and very low pitched sounds becomes weaker as their nerve endings deteriorate. This can be due to chronic ear infections or can simply be age related.

Your dog's ears have three parts: The outer or ear canal in which Max picks up sounds; the inner ear, which is separated by the tympanic membrane, which carries the sounds to the third part, the eardrum. The eardrum communicates the sounds to the nerve endings that carry them to the brain. Any of these parts can be affected by age-related illnesses or by lack of proper care. Ear damage is irreversible.

Ear Infections

This is the most common problem with both aged dogs and those with floppy ears. Infections can occur in the external or middle ear causing permanent damage. The cause of the infections can be bacteria, fungi, or yeast—all requiring different medications. Early symptoms may cause your dog to appear not to be listening well or he may not know when a new person has arrived in the room. The dog may show aggression when surprised.

Outer ear infection symptoms: Smelly discharge, constant shaking of the head, and rubbing his ear on solid objects such as door frames and furniture. Pain is also associated with ear infections. If the problem is mites, then a dark, granular discharge will be seen.

Treatment: Ear drops and ointments applied several times a day usually clear up the infection. In the case of ear mites, an anti-parasite medication will be used. Often, ear infections are associated with other ailments such as hypothyroidism.

Inner ear infection

symptoms: An afflicted dog may tilt his head to the side and his facial muscles will appear relaxed, similar to the symptoms of a stroke. If the infection progresses, the dog may show loss of equilibrium, circle around a lot, and twitch his eyeballs.

Treatment: High doses of drugs used to combat the infection as well as anti-inflammatory drugs will be administered to decrease the swelling. Flushing affected mucous out of the ear may be done to initiate the treatment. However, no matter how well the treatment proceeds, permanent hearing loss does result.

Adjustments: Make sure that Max is loose only in a fenced yard and walk him on a leash. Speak louder or stomp your feet to vibrate the ground when you want his attention. At night, you can get his attention by flicking lights on and off. When someone new comes, make it a point to introduce Max. Obedience training using hand and body language will be helpful when communicating with Max. He'll also enjoy learning new things. Just think of it...sign language with your dog!

SMELL

A dog's sense of smell may also deteriorate with age. Max's nose operates on two levels. The first level filters and warms the air before it reaches the respiratory tree. This is done by the turbanites fold in the nasal passages rich in blood vessels. The second function of the dog's nose is their incredible ability to detect the most minute odors. This ability to smell and differentiate odors has long been used in hunting, scenting activities such as search and rescue, narcotics detection, and obedience trials. Scent is the dog's prime means of differentiating people, places, and other animals. Dogs know the physiological and mental state of all living things that they detect. Can

Ear infections are common in older dogs and dogs with floppy ears. Keep your dog's ears clean and free of bacteria to avoid any problems.

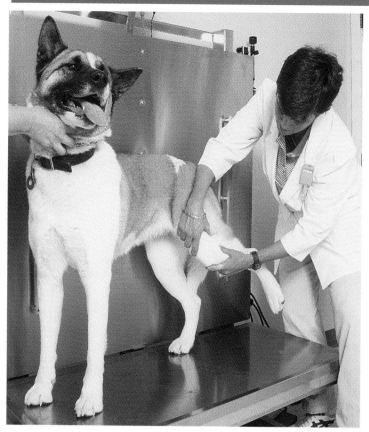

Your older dog's muscles and joints may be affected by diseases or illness. Good breeding, good diet, proper exercise, and regular checkups will help to keep him in shape.

foods. Heating his food also helps release a stronger aroma. Never allow Max to roam free because he has lost his ability to sense danger before it arrives, such as an aggressive dog or wild animal. Sometimes a dog without the ability to smell may become aggressive if surprised or in the presence of a stranger.

THE MUSCULOSKELETAL SYSTEM

The musculoskeletal system is composed of muscles, bones, and ligaments, as well as tendons. The entire system is built to withstand life's wear and tear. It will also show changes due to illnesses, cancer, and simple old-age-related syndromes such as arthritis and spondylosis. Muscle atrophy results from disuse due to pain and/or discomfort. Swelling can occur from arthritis, tumors, or injury. Changes in overall form such as a swelling abdomen, narrowing of the hips, or sagging of the muscles can be symptoms of a kidney or liver dysfunction. The worst case scenario can be a stroke or metastasized cancer.

Arthritis

This disease occurs in joints due to previous injury, age-related bone changes, or lack of specific nutrients throughout Max's life. Inflammation occurs when the synovial fluid—the fluid between the joints used to cushion the bones—increases production due to an overactive immune system that tries to lubricate an area due to abnormal bone changes.

Arthritis can occur in any

you imagine taking one whiff of something and knowing who left the odor, when they left it, and what they were thinking at the time? Incredible. Max's sense of smell is also closely associated with appetite. Thus, if he has nasal problems, he'll most likely not eat well.

Rhinitis

Rhinitis is caused by bacterial infections, tumors, foreign bodies, and exposure to toxic chemicals or trauma. Rhinitis is the most common age-related nasal dysfunction.

Symptoms: Nasal discharge, sneezing, and

gagging due to post-nasal drip.

Treatment: First, the veterinarian must determine if there is an underlying condition causing the problem. This is done through a physical examination, radiographs, and visual examination of the nasal passages. Often, in the case of infection, antimicrobial drugs, and anti-inflammatory drugs will be used. In the case of an obstruction, surgery can often restore complete sensory ability. However, age-related illnesses often result in permanent olfactory loss.

Adjustments: You can boost Max's appetite by offering stronger-smelling

As your dog shows signs of aging, try to keep him as happy and comfortable as possible. A mentally sound dog will stay physically sound much longer.

You can put the spring back in your dog's life by using a natural anti-inflammatory that eases arthritic joint symptoms and improves his mobility. Certain anti-inflammatories are specially formulated to help build and maintain healthy cartilage, tendons, and ligaments and aid in the regeneration of connective tissues in joints. Some products also include Grape Seed extract, an anti-oxidant to help control inflammation and discomfort. Photo courtesy of Francodex Laboratories, Inc.

joint, but is most prevalent in areas formally injured. Long-term infections can also cause arthritis. For example, a dog has repeated abscesses on his elbow. Within a few years, arthritis will develop in that elbow. This dysfunction can also be genetic, showing up as Max enters his senior years.

Treatment: Once diagnosed through radiographs and fluid evaluation, treatment often consists of anti-inflammatories, muscle relaxants, and the daily use of the nutriceuticals glycosamine sulfate and chondroitin, which help maintain a regular level of synovial fluid. Collagen is also used to maintain proper moisture and build up the cartilage around degenerating bones. While there is no cure for spinal arthritis, there is hope and surgery for arthritis of the hips and joints. Acupuncture and

chiropractic have also proven helpful in pain control.

Adjustments: Keep Max at a proper weight through diet and exercise. If he appears too stiff to exercise, still encourage him to do at least a little and the stiffness will subside. A proper diet is essential. There are now some great foods on the market that deliver a combination of proper ingredients for senior dogs as well as offer the nutriceuticals glycosamine and chondroitin.

Spondylosis

This disease involves the degeneration of the spinal cord and discs. Bony outgrowths appear along the spine and interfere with the nerves. While it is most common in larger breeds, medium-sized dogs are also prone to the degenerative effects. Occasionally, very old smaller dogs will succumb to spondylosis.

Symptoms: The dog may show no signs for years until the problem is very advanced. Initially, the dog may be stiff, then tend to fall a lot or be unable to stand on uneven ground. Eventually, the dog is paralyzed in the hind end.

Treatment: Once diagnosed with radiographs, anti-inflammatories are used to decrease the pain. Sometimes steroids injected directly into the afflicted area reduce swelling and allow more functionality. There is no cure.

Adjustments: You will need to allow Max more time to complete his daily routines. Keep him separate from other dogs so that he doesn't get jostled. He may tend to become more aggressive due to his pain, so be patient. Make sure you keep him on a low-fat, high-fiber diet so that he's not carrying around extra weight, which makes moving more difficult. Maintain some level of exercise, even if it's just a short walk around the block.

Metabolic Bone Disease

This dysfunction usually occurs when the kidney is malfunctioning. It is characterized by a thinning of the bone due to calcium being drawn out of the bone tissue to counteract the phosphorus rise in the blood calcium.

Symptoms: Lameness, overall weakness, bone deformities, and, when advanced, spontaneous fractures.

Treatment: Metabolic bone disease is first diagnosed through radiographs and blood tests. First, the kidney malfunction is addressed and treated. Then the bone disease

The best way to prevent your senior dog from suffering from diseases of the reproductive system is to have him spayed or neutered while young.

is treated with the administration of calcium supplements. Unfortunately, metabolic bone disease does progress and there is no cure.

Adjustments: Try to be patient and make your dog as comfortable as possible. Be certain to feed a high-calcium diet, as well as supplements. Don't allow Max to become obese, because this magnifies the problem.

Myositis

This is a common dysfunction in older dogs. The muscles become inflamed due to an infection or injury. Heart disease and poor circulation can also cause muscle inflammation.

The muscle cells actually break down and degenerate.

Symptoms: Max will be tender when touched and may cry or become aggressive. Muscle atrophy occurs because your dog does not want to use his sore areas. If the dysfunction advances, eating, drinking, and even breathing are affected.

Treatment: There is no cure. However, treatment with anti-inflammatory drugs can help ease the pain and discomfort. If there is an infection present, it can be treated with antibiotics.

Adjustments: Try to make Max as comfortable as possible. Serve moist, easy-

to-chew food, and keep him in a quiet, stress-free area.

REPRODUCTIVE SYSTEM

The best means of preventing problems in the reproductive system is to neuter or spay your dog. Old male dogs can suffer from perineal hernias, prostrate cancer, hormone imbalances, infections, and testicular cancer. Aged female dogs can also have hormone imbalances, infections, uterine cancer, pyometra, breast cancer, and ovarian cancer. You can prevent a lot of pain and heartache by removing the reproductive system of your pet.

Pyometra

This is an inflammation in

As dogs age, their level of activity decreases and their nutritional requirements change. There are dog foods available that are scientifically formulated to be nutritionally complete and balanced and provide energy, as well as promote healthy skin and coat. Photo courtesy of Midwestern Pet Foods, Inc.

the lining of the uterus. The uterus becomes distended with fluid and inflamed tissues. Pyometra can be caused by diabetes melitis, kidney malfunction, venereal disease, abnormal pregnancies or births, or from hormones used to prevent pregnancies.

Symptoms: Distended uterus, abnormal thirst, vomiting, and dehydration are all signs of pyometra. If the disease advances, the dog will have a fever and loss of appetite.

Treatment: First, the dog is neutered so that the disease cannot reoccur. Secondly, antibiotics and intravenous fluid is used to rehydrate the dog. This is a very serious

disorder in older dogs and, if not treated, can prove fatal.

Adjustments: Any dog over the age of seven should be neutered. If your dog becomes affected, seek immediate treatment. Once treated, allow your dog to rest in a stress-free environment. When Maxine is well, she can return to normal routines.

Prostrate Disorders

As male dogs age, they become susceptible to prostrate inflammation and infections. They are also prone to tumors, both malignant and benign. Either way, the dog becomes uncomfortable and has a difficult time passing urine.

Symptoms: Max will be

straining when he urinates and may have thin bloody stools, fever, abdominal pain, and weakness in the hind end. Recurring urinary tract infections also signify a prostrate problem.

Treatment: Once diagnosed through radiographs and urine analysis, if a tumor is present, it is removed. If the problem is due to an infection, then the dog is given antibiotics and the infected area is surgically drained. Neutering is done to prevent future problems.

Adjustments: Keep Max quiet for a while until he recovers. Once healed, he can return to his normal activities.

Hormonal Imbalances

This problem normally has an underlying cause, such as thyroid problems. The thyroid gland may be impacted, sending mixed messages to the hormone-producing organs.

Symptoms: Similar to thyroid symptoms, with abnormal hair loss, horrific skin odor, the skin becoming dark and thick, and Max becoming sensitive to the cold.

Treatment: Hormone imbalances are easily treated with replacement therapy and neutering.

Adjustments: Bathing your dog with special shampoo will stimulate hair growth and keep his skin soft. Daily "thyroid" pills will keep the problem under control. Max should maintain a normal activity level to keep his muscles strong and healthy.

URINARY SYSTEM

The urinary system is the most susceptible system to age-related dysfunction. In other words, it is most likely to be the first system to break down. This can begin with bladder infections or kidney dysfunction. Many older dogs may "leak" urine due to their sphincter muscles relaxing. This happens most often while the dog is asleep or playing.

The kidneys produce hormones that stimulate production of red blood cells, which regulate the blood pressure. If something goes wrong in the kidneys, the dysfunction can show symptoms in a number of ways.

Kidney Disease

The kidneys deteriorate with age. The tubules, which are the components in the kidneys that filter waste, become scarred and lose their function, putting greater stress on the other tubules. The stress works in on itself, causing further dysfunction and the inability to filter waste, which, in turn, poisons the dog's system.

Kidney problems can lead to other organ failures, as well as muscle atrophy and bone problems. The heart is pressured to work harder, creating abnormal blood flow. The kidneys slow down their production of red blood cells, which causes anemia and a reduction in oxygen carrying capacity, which leads to more heart stress. It is a vicious downhill cycle.

Symptoms: The symptoms do not generally show themselves until the kidney function is up to 70 percent lost. Dehydration, vomiting, distended abdomen, and if acute, unconsciousness, shock, and death.

Treatment: Once diagnosed through blood tests, the dog should receive plenty of water.

Weight maintenance, a frequent outdoor schedule, and plenty of fresh water will help your dog to avoid many elimination problems that may occur with old age.

While kidney disease cannot be cured and is a degenerative condition, there are special diets that can help slow the process, as well as medications to counteract the calcium deficiencies and ulcerations that might otherwise occur. Diuretics are also used to stimulate urine production. If there is any underlying sources of the kidney disease, such as periodontal infection, they are addressed and managed.

Adjustments: Allow Max access to fresh water at all times. Maintain his weight and feed him a low-fat, low-sodium, high-fiber diet. Try to make Max do some sort of exercise to stimulate his system.

Urinary Tract Infections

The urinary system will often work as a defense mechanism to keep bacteria away from the kidneys. The sphincters between the kidney, urethra, and bladder also work as a defense against spreading infection. The pH of the urine will change when infection has occurred.

Often, a urinary tract infection can be secondary to a worse problem, such as

With the proper treatment and care, even dogs that develop age-related illnesses can live out their senior years with dignity and in comfort.

to maintain a good body weight and along with eating a prescription diet low in sodium, fat, and sugar, he must have fresh water at all times. Max may need to take more trips outside to relieve himself. Allow him enough time to relieve himself several times each trip. If your dog is Maxine (female), keep the fur around her vulva trimmed short to discourage bacteria build-up.

A few other age-related problems that deserve mentions are Addison's disease, Cushing's disease, and diabetes. Addison's disease consists of a dysfunctional adrenal gland. It can be caused by inflammation, scarring, blood loss, or a tumor. The symptoms include muscle weakness, increased thirst, listlessness, or dull behavior. If the disease advances, the dog can suffer convulsions, shivering, and eventually, total collapse.

Cushing's disease occurs when the adrenal gland produces too many hormones due to a tumor in the pituitary or adrenal gland. Though most of the tumors in these areas are benign, they still cause inflammation and need to be removed. The symptoms include weakness, bulging eyes, increased appetite and thirst, bulging abdomen, and loss of coat. Cushing's disease is easily treated by removing the tumor or using medication to counteract the effects. Most dogs return to some semblance of normalcy, although they still need to be closely observed and allowed outside more often.

Diabetes occurs when age-related changes in the pancreas cause inadequate production of insulin. The

bacteria that gain entrance through internal and/or external organs that have undergone stress or dysfunction.

Symptoms: Frequent, painful urination is the most obvious symptom. Max will also be drinking more water than usual. Sometimes blood is present in the urine or the dog may be straining to urinate without success. Feeling sore, dogs may lick their urethral openings to soothe the areas. When the infection becomes

severe, the dog will have a fever, depression, and no appetite.

Treatment: Once the underlying causes are ruled out or taken care of, a round of antibiotics usually cures the problem. The antibiotics are administered for ten days to two weeks. For elderly dogs prone to repeated infections, the antibiotics may be administered daily at bedtime to build up in the urine overnight.

Adjustments: Max will need

blood sugar rises, causing sugar levels to rise in the urine. Thus, the sugar is not being fully absorbed by the body, causing insulin shock. A dog with diabetes will exhibit weight loss despite a good appetite. He'll drink more and urinate more as well. Treatment is usually a daily dose of insulin, as well as a high-fiber diet. Max will need to be watched carefully for secondary dysfunctions associated with diabetes, such as glaucoma, cataracts, pancreatitis, and other infections.

Diagnosis is easily done with a blood analysis and radiograph. There are medications available for all of these conditions. It is not known how fast or slow a dysfunction will advance. This may depend on outside influences such as proper diet, exercise, and low stress. Some dogs may live a good-quality life for years and others will suddenly suffer the acute symptoms of nausea, vomiting, and mental dullness, which inevitablly leads to death.

The best thing you can do for Max is to offer him a stress-free environment, fresh cool water, and frequent trips to his relief area. Try to maintain a balanced, sodium-free, high-fiber diet and make sure he gets plenty of exercise.

CARDIOVASCULAR DYSFUNCTION

Heart and lung problems are not common in older dogs and can be the most difficult problems to diagnose and treat. Due to advances in veterinary science, most of the causes of heart attacks, such

as heartworm infestation, can be prevented. However, germs can infiltrate the cardiovascular system through improper dental care, chronic bronchitis, emphysema, and fibrotic lung disease. Though they do occur, heart attacks are not common in canines.

Symptoms: Max may breathe rapidly or sound forced because he can't seem to catch his breath. He may be lethargic and tired, not wishing to exercise. A harsh cough can sometimes be symptomatic of a heart problem. If the condition worsens, you can detect a bluing of the tongue and absolute refusal to move.

Treatment: Once diagnosed through a blood test, radiographs, and a physical, most conditions are treated with medication. If the heart is unable to function on its own, a pacemaker can be installed. Proper diet is also helpful. There are ways to make your dog more comfortable, but there is no cure.

Adjustments: The best thing you can do is provide Max with a stress-free environment and don't allow him outside during extreme weather conditions. Make sure he gets some exercise and maintains a healthy weight.

Stroke

This occurs when the brain is suddenly deprived of oxygen through a blood clot or ruptured blood vessel in the brain. Strokes can often be mistaken for a seizure, especially in older dogs.

Symptoms: Aimless circling, crying, tilting of the

head, and pressing of the head against a solid object such as furniture or doors. Other symptoms include dragging a limb, a drooping face, and partial or complete paralysis. A massive stroke is fatal.

Treatment: There is no cure, but the veterinarian can give medications to reduce the swelling and remove excess fluid from the brain. A dog that suffers a mild stroke will require much nursing, such as being carried to his relief area, needing assistance in turning over and being spoon fed. However, within a few weeks he'll regain partial use of his limbs.

Adjustments: Max will have to be watched closely, because another stroke can occur at any time. He must be kept in a stress-free environ-ment and his movements should be restricted to a safely enclosed area.

DIGESTIVE SYSTEM DYSFUNCTIONS

The digestive system begins with the mouth and ends at the anus. There are miles of organs in between that are affected by many age-related ailments. The pancreas, liver, and gall bladder are accessories to the digestive system because they help with the creation of hormone production and enzymes to help break down foods and nutrients.

Because this system begins with the mouth, one should be very aware of proper dental maintenance to prevent periodontal disease, which is characterized by swollen gums, deteriorating teeth, and bad breath. If left untreated, it can cause tooth loss and

Large, deep-chested dogs can experience bloat, a condition that occurs when your dog eats too quickly. Be sure to monitor your dog's meals and limit his exercise after eating.

commonly when a dog eats too fast after rigorous exercise.

Bloat is caused by a build up of gases in the stomach, causing distention and the turning and twisting of the blood vessels, resulting in cutting off the blood flow. If not treated quickly, it can be fatal.

Symptoms: Gross abdominal enlargement and discomfort are the most obvious signs of bloat. A dog may dry heave continually and not be able to catch his breath.

Treatment: Max must be treated immediately. His stomach must be untwisted and tacked down. The gas must be extracted through a stomach tube or needle and medications administered to combat infection and shock. The prognosis is not always good because the condition can reoccur if not checked. If the dog survives his first week after the occurrence, he has a good chance of living through the experience. After recovery, surgery may be performed to permanently attach the stomach wall to the abdomen to prevent recurrence.

Adjustments: Always observe your dog after he exercises and eats. Feed him two to three smaller meals per day instead of one large one. Limit his water after meals and exercise. Also keep Max quiet for an hour and a half after his meals.

Liver Disease

The liver helps the digestive system process food by storing vitamins and nutrients and aiding in the breakdown of toxic by-products through its

secondary organ infections. Smaller dog breeds tend to be affected by this problem more often than larger dogs. A regular professional cleaning and scaling by a veterinarian will aid in preventing periodontal disease.

Proper diet is also important in preventing gum disease. A diet of meat and meat by-products has been know to lead to this disease. Older dogs should be fed at least some dry foods to help break down the plaque build-up on the gums and teeth.

Vegetables, such as carrots, will both help scrub the teeth and offer much needed vitamins. Those dogs with few teeth will need moist food and frequent brushings.

Bloat

This disease is often seen in deep-chested dogs such as German Shepherds, Weimaraners, Saint Bernards, and Rottweilers. However, it can be seen in those dogs who tend to eat too fast and are high strung, such as Jack Russell Terriers. Bloat occurs production of enzymes. Liver also helps remove old blood cells and process them, as well as produce bile acids that are stored in the gall bladder and secreted into the intestine to aid digestion.

When the liver is inflamed, the condition is called hepatitis. This can occur from diabetes melitis, infections, heart disease, poison, or malnutrition. If Max has repeated infections or assaults on the liver, a condition known as cirrhosis occurs. In this situation, scar tissue replaces liver tissue, decreasing the size of the organ and reducing its functionality.

Symptoms: Include a loss of appetite, diarrhea, vomiting, fever, jaundice, anemia, and distention of the abdomen. If the disease advances, seizures and death can result.

Treatment: Consists of first locating any underlying problems, and second, taking steps to control the symptoms, such as anti-vomiting medications, intravenous fluids, and, if the case has advanced to the point of anemia, blood transfusions. Once stabilized, the dog is put on regular antibiotics and a diet with high nutritional value. If Max continues not eating, he may be treated with an anabolic steroid to increase his appetite and metabolism.

Colitis

This is a common ailment in aging dogs. It can happen off and on, depending on the dog's diet and stress level. It can also be caused by polyps, tumors, foreign bodies such as parasites, or

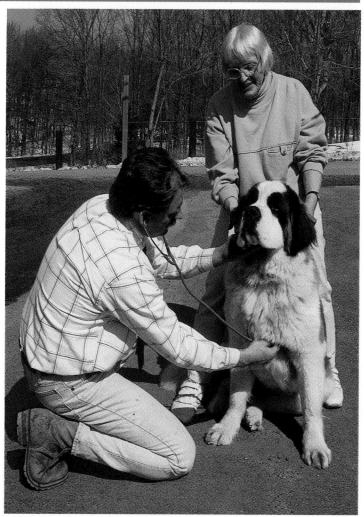

Many diseases that affect aging dogs are stress related. A calm and happy home environment combined with good veterinary care will help keep your dog healthy.

immune system disorders.

Symptoms: Colitis is identified by loose, bloody, and/or mucousy stool.

Treatment: Once diagnosed through endoscopy, if there is an obstruction, it is removed. If the colitis is caused by simple intestinal dysfunction, the dog is put on medication, such as antibiotics. Often the medication need only be administered for a short period, such as ten days.

Should the colitis again appear, then the medicine is used again.

Adjustments: Max should be kept on a bland diet that is high in fiber. He should also live in a stress-free environment, because stress can cause colitis to reoccur.

ALLERGIES

According to Chris Pinny, D.V.M. in his book, *Caring for Your Older Dog*, "An allergy is caused by an exaggerated immune response to a foreign substance within or on the surface of the body."

As Max ages, his entire system will become more sensitive to his environment. Pollen, toxins, and parasites will affect him more than when he was younger. The thinning of his coat, along with a disruption in his shedding processes, allow the environment to affect his skin. The sebum or oil secretions formally used to lubricate his coat no longer help his fur keep fungi and bacteria away from his skin. Internal dysfunctions often show themselves in a dry, flaky coat.

Skin allergies can also occur when a dog is younger. These are usually allergies to inhalants, such as pollen. Flea allergies can also manifest themselves while the dog is young and become so bad that he loses his fur. Contact allergies, such as reactions to detergents, insecticides, or bedding can also erupt as Max ages.

Symptoms: Small reddish bumps on the skin and constant rubbing of the nose and licking of paws or affected areas. Discomfort and thickening of the skin are also symptoms.

Treatment: Depending on the type of allergy, special shampoos can be used to relieve dermal itching. Anti-inflammatory drugs and steroids are used to reduce swelling. Antihistamines can be used if Max has an inhalant allergy. Due to the detrimental effects of long-term steroid usage, especially in older dogs, it's best to first discover the reason behind the allergy and make sure the dog isn't in contact with this irritation. Vitamin E is also helpful in maintaining moisture and elasticity in the skin.

Adjustments: You may have to change Max's bedding to something hypoallergenic. His shampoo and other topical treatments also need to be hypoallergenic. Keeping him free of fleas is the best means of ensuring that he remains healthy both inside and out. Max may need to go on a special prescription food to avoid further allergic reactions to food substances. Allergic reactions are highly treatable and once Max is on a normal maintenance plan, he will return to a good quality of life.

Cancer

The tendency of tumors to occur, both benign and malignant, increases as dogs age. Cancer can occur in any tissue or organ and develop quickly without any outward symptoms until it's too late. Some tumors are operable and have a good prognosis, such as skin tumors. Others are not, such as cancer of the liver.

Skin cancer is the most common type of cancer in older dogs. It is characterized by a hard, lumpy growth. It needs to be removed immediately. Tumors in the urinary system are characterized by blood in the urine. Tumors in the gastrointestinal tract are characterized by bloody stool and straining as the dog defecates. Brain or spinal cord tumors, whether benign or malignant, can cause severe behavioral abnormalities such as sudden aggression or constant crying.

Symptoms: Once cancer has spread through the body, the dog's muscles appear to atrophy. He may become thin, and look as though he's wasting away. Depending on the type of cancer, his stomach may look distended, while the rest of him appears skeletal. He'll have trouble relieving himself and may refuse to eat. Often, his skin will give off an offensive odor.

Treatment: Once diagnosed through radiographs, ultrasound, and blood tests, the dog can be treated provided the cancer has not metastasized. The treatment usually consists of removal of the tumor, then chemotherapy, and/or radiation therapy. The prognoses is good, provide the entire tumor has been removed.

Adjustments: Once Max has had a cancerous tumor, he may be prone to more. He will need to see his veterinarian regularly and have yearly blood tests to ensure nothing else has occurred. If he feels up to it, offer him regular exercise and a diet low in sugar and fats and high in fiber.

While older dogs may be more susceptible to disease and allergens, this does not mean that they cannot have a good-quality life. It simply means that you need to be more observant of Max's behavior both while he's active and while he's asleep. Anything that strikes you as different may be the early sign of a problem. You should immediately take him to your veterinarian and have the symptom(s) checked. Waiting until a problem worsens can make it more difficult to treat.

FUN WITH OLD FRIENDS

Provided he is healthy, Max will be able to do anything a younger dog can do. Dogs aren't aware that they are old and some maintain an active lifestyle even if they suffer from the early stages of a dysfunction such as arthritis or kidney disease. Unlike people, dogs age gracefully, not worried about a few gray hairs or the loss of fur. They don't care about a few calluses at the elbows or teeth that are no longer full and bright.

As long as Max has the energy level and desire to exercise, he should be given time each day to do so. Exercise promotes a healthier and longer life, as well as helps you relieve yourself of the daily stresses. What can be more fun than going for a run or playing ball with your best friend? Worries? Cares? They're gone in a flash of Max's grin and wag of his tail.

Never make up excuses to avoid that walk around the block or run through the park. Weather conditions and your own exhaustion from work mean nothing to a dog that has maintained this routine his entire life. In fact, as Carl Gorman states in his book, *The Aging Dog*, one of the major benefits of having a dog is that it forces us to keep ourselves in shape.

Exercise and stimulation keep our pets' minds occupied and bodies healthy. A dog that only lies around soon becomes overweight and lethargic. His life is dull, offering little or no

Provided he is healthy, your older dog should be able to do anything a younger dog can do. Eighteen-year-old Brutus can nap with the best of them.

As long as your senior dog has the energy level and desire, he should be given the opportunity to exercise and play every day.

even if the other dog only looks at him the wrong way. A cranky dog should only be with others on neutral territory and not with dogs that may have dominant personalities. Max has earned his place as top dog and doesn't need the stress of being challenged.

As a regular routine, Max should be allowed outside for at least 20 minutes of exercise twice a day. This exercise time can consist of a walk, play time, or training time. Yes, dogs still should be trained when they are old because they enjoy the mind stimulation. If Max becomes stiff the next day, reduce your walking speed or the amounts of time you make him change positions. Allow him to perform his commands at a slower pace. Be patient. It takes a little longer for those old bones to work.

If Max has severe arthritis or a heart condition, he can still benefit from walking down to the mailbox and back. He'll enjoy sniffing the air and listening to the sounds of nature. He'll most enjoy spending the time with you. The golden years are when we take time to smell the roses.

The types of exercise depend largely on Max's condition. As he ages, he'll be prone to arthritis and more susceptible to injury, so you don't want to make him perform the same duties as when he was younger. For example, he may have run with you five miles per day. One morning, he wakes up a bit stiff. He can't do the same distance anymore. Begin reducing the distance and

stimulation. This alone can cause a dog's body to break down. Obesity can either cause or exacerbate already existing conditions. Dogs also need an occasional change in atmosphere. This can consist of playing with him at the park or simply walking with him down the street. Daily walks or exercise times give Max something to look forward to.

The ideal type of exercise for a senior dog is being allowed to play with other dogs. It will put new life in

Max, making him feel young at heart. However, the amount of exercise and with whom depends on his state of health. You don't want to put Max in with a bunch of rambunctious pups if he has advanced arthritis or is recovering from surgery. You'll also want to make sure that Max wants the company. Often, as dogs age, they become senile and cranky. The presence of another dog in his special spot, for example, may cause Max to become aggressive, when even that causes stiffness, slow down the gait. It might help to run on a softer surface. When even that proves too much, do the exercise at a walk. Walking is less jarring, offering low impact aerobic conditioning while continuing the maintenance of good muscle tone.

If Max has been involved in obedience or agility, he can still perform these things, only the obstacles will need to be lowered to accommodate him. Max loves doing these exercises and you should still offer him the opportunity, just make sure it doesn't harm him in the long run. For example, lower a jump height or reduce the amount of times you expect him to change his body position. Older dogs can perform a stay exercise far better than a younger dog, so while you work with a younger sibling, have Max do a long stay. This is equally beneficial, because Max is happily working while providing a distraction for the younger dog.

Retrieving exercises will also need to be toned down a bit. While Max used to love jumping up for his ball, this can cause injuries later in life that may lead to chronic arthritis and joint pain. Instead of having Max retrieve his ball in the air, roll it along the ground. Another way to avoid injury during a game of fetch is to teach Max to remain in a stay until the ball stops moving, then allow him to retrieve it. This way he isn't twisting and jumping after it, if it ricochets off a tree or fence.

Swimming is the ideal exercise for older dogs. It not only exercises sore joints, but actually builds the muscles around them. This

Swimming is the ideal exercise for senior dogs because it exercises the joints and muscles without straining them. This Great Dane and Doberman share the fun of water retrieval.

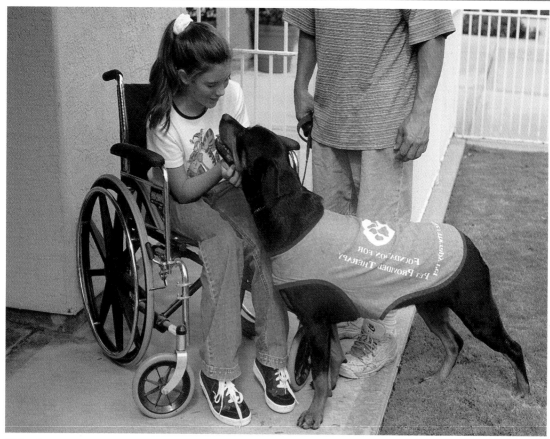

Older dogs are perfect for therapy work. Their calm demeanors and loving manners can bring joy to many people.

alleviates much of the pain associated with arthritis. Best of all, if Max is a sporting, herding, or working dog, he will thoroughly enjoy it. He'd especially be more eager to swim if he saw other dogs doing the same. Take the entire pack out for a day at the lake, or if you're lucky enough to have a swimming pool, let Max make use of it. You can do fetch-the-stick relays!

ACTIVITIES FOR AGED DOGS

There are many jobs Max can perform better as an older dog than he could as a bouncy puppy. One of these is therapy work. This consists of going into nursing homes, hospitals, and retirement villages to offer the residents the love and comfort of your wonderful dog. Many of these people had to give up their own beloved pets, and Max will give them a moment of fond memories. Not only will it liven up the residents' lives, but Max will have a great time getting scratched and fussed over. How many dogs would not look forward to that? Max will be anxiously waiting at the door!

For Max to become a therapy dog, he must first receive basic obedience training so that he will sit still as he is being fawned over. He must also learn that jumping up is forbidden, as is rushing into people.

Learning how to perform the down/stay command will also be helpful when being touched by children or the infirm.

A few other tricks that may be helpful to teach him are to lay his head in a lap, shake, and fetch things. While these tricks may be natural for many dogs, others will need to be taught. Before starting anything, always begin with the basics—Heel, Sit, Stay, Down, Come, and Stand. Once Max can perform these commands in the company of others, you can teach him anything. Most dogs will already know these behaviors and just need a little refresher course. Max will love going with you to a

Basic obedience training while young is the stepping stone your senior dog needs to continue using his abilities. This rescue Lab proudly shows off the fruits of his labor.

Teaching your dog tricks is a great way to keep your older dog in training practice and his skills sharp. This Rottweiler performs the "shake" with his mistress.

pawing at your leg. A therapy dog should not be allowed to do this because he can damage sensitive skin. However, he should be able to place his paw gently into someone's outstretched hand.

Begin by placing Max in a sit/stay. Turn and face him. Put a treat in one hand and bring his head to the side opposite the paw you wish to lift. As he moves to sniff the treat, he will be taking his weight off the other leg. At this time, tap his leg with your other hand as you say, "Shake." As soon as his leg moves, praise and give him the treat. Each time you ask for the Shake, require him to move his leg a little more. As he learns to actually pick up his foot, make him lift it higher and higher before giving him his reward. Always praise him as he responds. This encourages him to perform. You have completed the trick when Max will gently lay his paw in your outstretched hand. Imagine the smiles he'll bring to many faces!

The fetching trick only works on dogs that are already predisposed to the activity. If Max does not already fetch, you will only make him frustrated if you begin teaching him as a senior. The last thing you want to do is hurt or stress him in any way. Try another trick instead, such as rolling over. This is easily done by first putting Max in a down/stay. Show him a bit of food and bring his head toward his back. As he reaches for the treat, his body will roll itself. Each time you ask for the behavior, require more

weekly obedience lesson and showing off to those young upstarts who drag their owners about. He might even teach them a thing or two.

The easiest new behavior for Max to learn and the one that will earn him much affection is placing his head in a lap or the "I'm so cute, you must pet me," trick. This is easily done with a bit of food. Begin by placing Max in a sit/stay next to a chair. Sit in the chair and show him the food. Draw his attention to your lap by placing the food there. When his nose is

stretching toward your lap, praise him and let him have the food. Each time he comes closer to your lap, give him his reward. Always require more and more response from him before he gets the food. Before you know it, his head is in your lap and he's getting the food himself. As soon as he can do this, begin stroking his head and praising him. Max will soon relax his head in your lap, enjoying your affection.

The next trick is the shake. Many dogs naturally try to draw your attention by movement. You can gently help him to roll the first couple times. He'll soon understand what you want and will eagerly perform the trick. Always offer lots of praise and affection when he does as you ask.

For those dogs that like to fetch, bring a soft toy with you when you do therapy visits. Residents will clap with delight as Max plays retrieving games with them. Max will need to learn, however, exactly where to return the toy. Many residents are unable to bend over and pick things up. The toy needs to be returned to the person's lap or hands. To teach this, require Max to bring the toy closer and closer to the target area before throwing it for him. Each time he brings it closer, praise and offer a treat or pet him. It won't take him long to figure out what you want. Being a senior dog has its advantages. Foremost is Max's ability to understand you. If your dog has earned obedience or agility titles, there are special classes for senior dogs in which Max can compete. Veteran's class is a non-regular class similar to Novice at an obedience trial. The dog must heel on and off leash, perform a figure eight around two people, stay and come off lead, stand still while being examined by the judge, and remain in a sit/stay for one minute and a down/stay for three minutes as the handler stands 30 feet away. You can be pretty sure that few of these veterans move during their stay exercises. Some kennel clubs also offer a veteran's Open class. This

This Cocker Spaniel has still got it! Agility shows cater to the senior dog by providing special competitions that are fun for the dogs and the spectators.

offers the opportunity for Max to jump, retrieve, drop on a recall, and perform long stays with his handler out of sight. The jumps are lower than normal Open classes to

Retractable leashes provide dogs freedom while allowing the owner complete control. Leashes are available in a wide variety of lengths for all breeds of dogs. Photo courtesy of Flexi-USA, Inc.

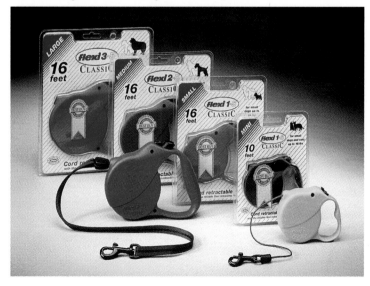

For some older dogs, a walk in the woods or down the block can be just as stimulating as organized dog sports. This is Devon, owned by Adrienne Rescinio.

accommodate the senior competitors.

Conformation shows will often have a showcase of past winners that parade through the ring, once again strutting their stuff. Some shows offer senior conformation classes. Many well-bred dogs continue to earn points and titles well into their teens. Even Westminster, the greatest conformation show in the nation, offers a parade of past winners. Most senior dogs are very excited about being fussed over and strutting like the youngsters in the next ring. Senior show dogs need never retire unless they begin to show disinterest or have a debilitating dysfunction.

Agility also caters to senior dogs with special competitions. The jumps and obstacles require less athletic ability, but still challenge your dog. You can set up your own agility course in your backyard using boards. Lay one wooden board across the ground to use as a narrow walkway. Place one on a small pedestal to make a see-saw. Prop a board against two chairs or closely spaced trees as a jump. Use two chairs or small cones for weave poles. These props may not be as pretty as the gaily painted agility obstacles, but theycan be lots of fun for you and Max.

A walk in the woods can

prove just as stimulating as an agility course. You can place Max on a sit/stay in a heavily treed area and go a short distance away. Call him to come. He'll have to weave through the trees to come to you. Downed trees also make great jumps. Just be sure that the trail is not too strenuous for Max's condition and always bring plenty of water.

Another activity that offers lots of stimulation and is not overly stressful is tracking. While many of the dog's senses such as sight and hearing degenerate with age, their sense of smell usually remains very strong. Tracking offers the stimulation of discovery as well as the thrill of performing.

Teaching a dog to track is one of the easiest things to teach because you are working with their natural predatory instincts. This activity can be started in your home by teaching Max to find a treat. Begin by placing the treat in plain sight and then allowing Max to go eat it. Next, place the treat partially out of sight and then send Max for his food. When he quickly retrieves his reward, place it out of sight. Now Max has to search for his reward. As Max advances, place the treat in more and more difficult places. Max must use his nose to locate the food.

When Max is adept at finding the food, you can transfer his task to locating an object, such as a wallet or sock. To do this, simply place the treat on the object. Soon, Max will locate the object without your having to put a treat on top of it. When he finds something, be sure to let him know how good he is and praise him. Next, teach Max to bark, whine, or come back to you to let you know he's found something. This is easily taught by getting him excited when he's located the object. As soon as he exhibits excitement, give him his reward.

If Max is able to work outside, you can begin increasing the distances and

difficulty of his track and adding more objects. Many old dogs are entered in tracking events and, due to their decreased susceptibility to distraction, often do very well. A dog can track until he can no longer walk.

Another job in which senior dogs excel is media or production work. Max could be an animal actor! Older dogs tend to have character, something that is greatly needed when doing a commercial or advertisement. Many dogs that can no longer perform in the obedience ring can still do well in front of a camera.

An animal actor must be photogenic. This means that

Another activity that older dogs excel in is media and production work. A well-trained, well-groomed, healthy-looking dog can easily be a star.

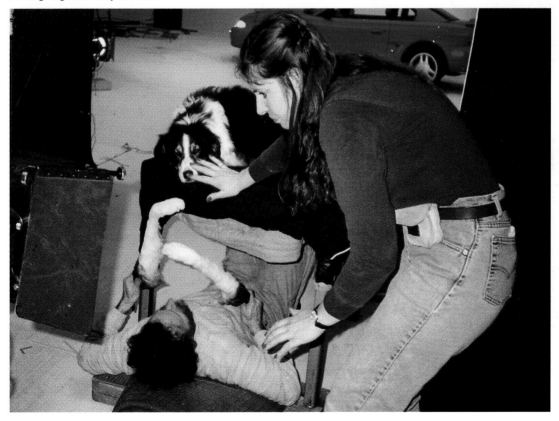

A senior dog can make a loving and loyal friend. If you take special care of your aging dog, you will be rewarded with his company for many years to come.

his eyes should be expressive and body in good condition. Until your dog is geriatric he can remain in peak condition—shiny coat and teeth and at the proper weight. Dogs with spots or multicolors show up great on film. Yellow dogs, such as Labrador and Golden Retrievers, as well as some hound breeds are very photogenic. Terriers are full of expression, hence their popularity in movies. There are also many mixed breeds that add a distinction all their own.

Besides being in good health, animal actors must be able to perform at least the basic commands and respond quickly to both visual and verbal cues from a distance with any type of distraction. This requires extensive training. If Max is already an accomplished obedience trial dog, he'll fit right in as an animal actor. Many therapy dogs will also work well in front of the camera. However, if he has not performed in these arenas, in order to properly prepare Max for a job as an animal actor, you must first complete both on- and off-leash obedience training and he needs to be able to ignore distractions.

While knowing the basics will get a paw in the door, knowledge of special tricks will get Max noticed. More often than not, a canine actor will be required to hold things in his mouth, bark on command, wear silly outfits, and work long hours. Moreover, he'll have to ignore people and most likely other animals from antelopes to zebras. An animal actor must learn to watch only his handler and not be distracted by anything. Costumers primp and directors want a minor body part moved just a fraction of an inch as the shot is being set up. There are hot lights and people rushing by. Max must not only endure this with good humor, but look forward to returning to the same spot for another 30 takes. This requires a very special dog.

Most animal actors thoroughly enjoy their work because they receive lots of attention and treats. Max will feel very important as people fawn over him and praise his good looks. Veteran animal actors will peruse the set prior to going into action so that they can say hello and visit.

Old dogs are our best friends. They wish only to be part of our lives, remain stimulated, and to feel needed. There is never any reason to let them fall by the wayside and be forgotten. Max wishes only to be with you and please you, no matter what you do. Offer him the quality of life that you would seek for yourself, and you will be rewarded with Max's quiet company for many years to come.